Original title:
Botany in Ballads



Author: Benjamin Caldwell
ISBN HARDBACK: 978-1-80567-035-3
ISBN PAPERBACK: 978-1-80567-115-2

## Evensong of the Eucalyptus

In the tree tops, koalas snooze,
While eucalyptus tips play the blues.
Leaves sway gently in a dance,
Nature's perfume, a leafy romance.

Squirrels giggle, searching for snacks,
While wise old owls keep tally of tracks.
Whispers of leaves in the dusk's embrace,
Eucalyptus antics, a hilarious chase.

## Verses of the Verdant Vale

In the vale where sunbeams smile,
Flowers prance in vibrant style.
Bees are buzzing with sweet delight,
Life's a game, not just a fight.

Bouncing bunnies in a race,
Hide and seek with clover's grace.
With every bloom a tale is spun,
In the vale, we laugh and run.

## Scented Stories

Roses giggle with their thorny pride,
While daisies do a polka slide.
Lavender whispers, 'Have a ball!',
Scented tales, they enthrall us all.

Tulips twirl in the airy glow,
Bright to dull, then back to show.
Each blossom boasts a silly wit,
In scented stories, we never quit.

## The Lilt of Loam

Soil sings softly, a deep, rich tune,
As worms waltz under the silver moon.
Roots play tag beneath the ground,
In laughter, the echoes all around.

Frogs croak jokes near the pond,
While crickets chirp their dreams so fond.
Every inch of earth’s a stage,
With loam's lilt, we engage.

## Echoes of Elderflower

In the garden where flowers chat,
Elderflower wears a silly hat.
Bees buzz tunes quite off-key,
Dancing wildly, oh what a spree!

Their petals shake in laughter bright,
As raindrops fall, a comical sight.
With every sip of elder's brew,
The wittiest blooms say, "Cheers to you!"

A rabbit hops, tries to twirl,
But trips on roots, poor little girl.
The daisies giggle, they can’t resist,
For nature's punchlines are hard to miss!

So gather 'round in this flowery nest,
For elderflower's humor is simply the best.

## A Tale of Thorny Trials

In a garden filled with poky foes,
Thorns planned pranks, as everyone knows.
Rose thought herself a queen of grace,
But cactus yelled, "Look at this face!"

With prickly jokes that pierced the air,
The thorns would plot without a care.
“Is this a flower or a hedge?” they'd tease,
As daisies chuckled in the breeze.

One day a sapling tried to climb,
Only to fall in a messy rhyme.
“I’m not thistled about the fall!”
Yelled the apple tree, “Let’s share the call!”

Through thorny tales and laughter loud,
They bloomed in chaos, proudly unbowed.

## The Harp of Hanging Gardens

In the hanging gardens, melodies grew,
With vines that danced and flowers that flew.
The lilies strummed a joyful tune,
While marigolds swayed, under the moon.

A foggy foghorn called for a song,
But crickets chirped, all night long.
"Are we a band or just a mess?"
Laughed the orchids, dressed to impress!

The beans took turns on a leafy stage,
While sunflowers read from a plant-based page.
With laughter and fun, they all played along,
Creating a heartwarming, silly song.

Oh, the harp of gardens clung tight to the sun,
In this botanical ballad, everyone's won!

## The Enchantment of Everleaf

Once in a realm of everleaf green,
A plant had a secret, rarely seen.
It giggled softly, shared its charm,
Enticing all with a leafy arm.

In the twilight, amid shadows cast,
It tickled the toes of critters fast.
"Wanna join my leafy dance?" it said,
With all the flowers bouncing ahead!

The ferns whispered jokes, quite absurd,
While gourds and squashes scampered, unheard.
They twirled and laughed, a joyous train,
As petals spun, swirling down the lane.

So join the fun in this leafy field,
Where enchantment blooms, and laughter is healed.

## In Praise of Petal Poetry

Oh petals dance like tiny shoes,
They twirl and spin, they sing the blues.
In gardens vast, they strut their stuff,
With colors bright, they're never gruff.

In springtime's breeze, they burst with glee,
They giggle at bees, saying, "Come sip me!"
A daisy's wink, a rose's sigh,
They pen a poem, oh my, oh my!

## The Melody of Mossy Mornings

In a damp green cloak, the moss does hum,
It tickles the toes, oh what a bum!
Beneath the trees where shadows play,
The moss is king, hip-hip-hooray!

With every step on its fuzzy bed,
It whispers secrets, fills hearts with dread.
"Watch your step!" it warns with glee,
For slipping sounds like pure comedy.

## Stanzas from the Secret Meadow

In a meadow wild, the flowers meet,
They gossip and giggle, oh what a treat!
The violets tease the shy buttercup,
"You're so bashful, come cheer up!"

The daisies laugh, they roll and play,
While bumblebees buzz in their funny way.
Their silly antics, a floral show,
In nature's play, they steal the glow.

## The Chronicle of the Cactus

A cactus stood tall with prickles galore,
It said to the sun, "Come on, give me more!"
With arms stretched wide, it waved hello,
"I'm the spikiest star in this desert show!"

It tells tall tales of the heat it bears,
Of quirky critters and prickly hares.
With laughter and charm, it's never blue,
A funny green friend, always true.

## The Ballad of Blooming Shadows

In the garden a shadow, with petals so bright,
It danced in the moonlight, a comical sight.
A bee tried to flirt, but it toppled and fell,
The flowers all giggled, oh what a swell!

With a wink and a nod, it swayed with delight,
The daisies all chuckled, it felt really right.
A scarecrow nearby shook his head with disdain,
'The blooms with no sense are driving me insane!'

## Ode to the Ancient Arbor

Oh ancient tree, with branches so wide,
Your roots hold the secrets where gnomes like to hide.
You shed all your leaves, like a clumsy old man,
'Trust me,' said the squirrel, 'it was part of the plan!'

With acorns like cannonballs, fallen with glee,
You laugh as the children climb high on your knee.
Yet when autumn arrives, and your colors take flight,
You boast, 'I am the sunset, I'm the star of the night!'

## The Curiosity of Climbing Vines

Oh, the climbing vines, with their whimsical spree,
They twirl and they tangle, oh what a sight to see!
They stretch for the sky, with mischievous cheer,
'Excuse us,' says the ivy, 'we're just getting here!'

A trellis they conquered, with grip so profound,
As they wrapped around turtles who didn't make a sound.
'You're not a snail, but we'll make you our friend,'
Laughed the vines on the turtles, their journey to bend!

## The Portrait of Pollen

Oh pollen, you rascal, so light on the breeze,
You tickle the noses of folks if you please.
With a wink and a wave, you dance through the air,
Leaving sneezes behind, but no one seems to care!

A dandelion puff, like a fluffy parade,
You joke with the wind, 'I'm not really afraid!'
But when flowers all blush, it's an artful display,
Mocking bees buzzing, oh what a ballet!

## An Anthem for the Almond Trees

Oh almond trees, you stand in rows,
With nuts so bold, putting on shows.
Your blossoms dance in springtime air,
While bees declare, "We're nuts, we swear!"

In summer sun, your branches sway,
As squirrels plan their grand buffet.
A feast of nuts, oh what a sight,
They munch and munch, with sheer delight!

When autumn comes, your bounty falls,
The ground is filled with crunching calls.
While folks in towns begin to pine,
For almond treats, a treat divine!

So raise a glass to trees so grand,
With nuts that tickle every hand.
An anthem sung in joyful cheer,
To almond trees, we hold so dear!

## The Saga of the Sagebrush

Oh sagebrush brave, you stand so tall,
In desert lands, you grow for all.
Your scent, it wafts through winds that swirl,
A fragrant plume in nature's whirl!

With roots that dig and stretch so wide,
You hold the soil, our faithful guide.
While lizards lounge, and rabbits play,
You shade them well in bright array.

When rain does come, you drink it up,
Your thirsty thirst, a flower cup.
But when it's dry, you keep your grace,
A sage-like stance in barren place!

So here's to you, dear sagebrush friend,
On you, the desert relies and depends.
Your tale we tell with laughter bright,
In arid lands, you're pure delight!

## Chants of Climbing Roses

Oh climbing roses, up you go,
With petals bright, you steal the show.
You twist and turn on fences high,
A floral climb to touch the sky!

In morning light, you smile and gleam,
While bees are buzzing in a dream.
You flirt with walls, a bold romance,
In gardens where the pollens dance!

A gentle vine, you’re full of charm,
But thorns do warn, "Don’t cause alarm!"
For every kiss, there’s prickly jest,
A garden's joke we can't contest!

So here’s to you, dear roses fair,
In nature’s jest, you steal the air.
Your climbing song, we’ll gladly sing,
With petals soft, you are the king!

## The Song of Soil

Oh soil beneath, you're full of dreams,
With worms and bugs, like nature's teams.
You hold the secrets of each sprout,
A muddy mix that sings about!

In gardens rich, you do your part,
With roots that dig and worms that dart.
You take the scraps and turn them grand,
Transforming waste to nourish land!

When rain does fall, you soak it in,
A spongy bed where life begins.
With every seed that touches ground,
You whisper songs where life is found!

So raise your voice, oh humble dirt,
With laughter loud, let's sing alert.
For every plant that grows on you,
The song of soil will ring so true!

## Whispers of the Garden's Heart

In the garden, flowers giggle,
Roses blush when bumblebees wiggle.
Tulips whisper secrets at dawn,
While daisies dance on the lawn.

Sunflowers grin, with heads so tall,
Pansies chuckle, but not for all.
The grapevine laughs, tangled and sweet,
As carrots tickle the little feet.

Bees share jokes with the buzzing breeze,
Every leaf rustles with playful tease.
The marigold claps with golden cheer,
And even the weeds join in the sneer.

So come along, sit by the greens,
Join the mischief of simple scenes.
For in this realm where laughter's king,
Every twig holds a song to sing.

## The Sonnet of the Swaying Willow

There once was a willow, so tall and swish,
It wobbled and danced with every swish.
The squirrels would mock, play tricks in its shade,
While crickets chirped songs, as if they had played.

The branches would bow, then spring back with sass,
As if they were ballerinas, showing off class.
With every light breeze, it sighed and it swung,
Each leaf a sweet note in the chorus it sung.

One day it pretended to sweep up the ground,
Then tossed all its leaves, which caused quite a sound.
“Oops!” it exclaimed, “Was that really me?"
The laughter from neighbors was joyful and free.

So sway, oh dear willow, don’t let your woes,
Become heavy burdens with all of the throes.
For life in the garden is meant to be fun,
Let loose, spin about, and soak up the sun!

## Petals and Parables

In a patch where violets plot and plan,
Petals gossip like a well-aged fan.
They swap their wishes and twirl about,
In stories spun with joy and pouts.

A daffodil told of a brave little bee,
Who buzzed through the air, wild and free.
The rose rolled her eyes, "Oh what a plight!"
Yet all agreed it was pure delight.

In the shadowed corners where daisies thrive,
They shared tall tales of how they survive.
"Watch out for gnomes!" one piped with a grin,
"They'll steal all your blooms and dance on your skin!"

So let the petals share their fondest dreams,
Life in the garden is not what it seems.
With every laugh, and each twist of fate,
Nature's tales flourish, we celebrate!

## Lullabies of Leafy Lore

Underneath the old oak, wise and wide,
The raccoons host parties, full of pride.
With mushrooms as tables and acorns for chairs,
They toast to the moon, while no one quite stares.

The ferns softly murmur their evening song,
While fireflies twinkle and hum right along.
"Let's play hide and seek!" shouts a spry little sprout,
And soon laughter ripples all about.

Night blooms unfold with a flutter and flit,
Each petal a dancer, each bud a bright skit.
The stars twinkle back with a wink and a nod,
As if they're all praising the ground and the sod.

In this world of whimsy, where all things grow,
Life's a lush carpet of sprightly tableau.
So cuddle your roots and rest your sore knees,
In the lullabies sung by the rustling leaves.

## Crescendo of the Chrysanthemums

In the garden, blooms so bright,
Chrysanthemums dance with delight.
They shimmy and sway in the breeze,
Whispering secrets to buzzing bees.

Their petals like skirts, twirling around,
As butterflies flutter without a sound.
A flower parade with colors so grand,
Even gnomes rock out with a band!

Each yellow and pink, a laugh in the sun,
Nature's own party, a glorious fun.
With a wink and a wiggle, they tease and they play,
Chrysanthemums rule in their floral ballet!

So come take a peek, don’t be shy,
Join in the laughter, give it a try.
In this garden of whimsy, life’s a fancy romp,
Where blooms throw a bash, and the roots play the tromp!

## Harmonious Hedges

A row of hedges in shades of green,
Whispering tunes, a leafy scene.
They gossip and giggle, sprouting their leaves,
Sharing the juiciest tales as they weave.

One hedge claims it’s wiser than the last,
Telling stories of seasons that have passed.
With trim little tops and sides so neat,
They argue on who’s served the best treat!

The neighborly flowers poke fun at their fuss,
Saying, 'Hedges, chill out! Don’t make a big fuss!'
But the hedges just hum their melodious tune,
Swaying gently under the light of the moon.

The gardener chuckles, giving a nudge,
'Keep singing, my friends; don't let the fun budge!'
These hedges unite in harmony sweet,
A quirky ensemble, with talent to greet!

## The Narrative of Nectar

In a flower's heart, a tale unfolds,
Where nectar flows like treasures untold.
Bees gather 'round with a mischievous buzz,
Each droplet a secret, each drop a buzz!

A daisy declares, 'I'm the sweetest around!'
While roses blush red, feeling quite proud.
But the humble dandelion, with charm so small,
Claims, 'I'm the queen; I'm loved by them all!'

With every sip, there's laughter and cheer,
As pollinators dance, spreading joy near.
Each drop tells a joke, a funny little tale,
As the flowers giggle and sway without fail.

So join in this feast, where the humor flows,
Nectar-filled stories, every petal knows.
In nature's own party, the fun's never done,
Where every little bloom shines bright in the sun!

## Petal's Persuasion

Petals gathered ‘round for a chat,
'How do we charm? What’s the cool cat?'
One shouts, 'Let’s sparkle with colors so nice!'
While another suggests a dance that’s precise.

With a wiggle and jiggle, they start to flirt,
Swirling and twirling, oh, what a spurt!
They toss out sweet scents, a fragrant delight,
Each trying to woo bees swooping in flight.

A sunflower laughs, 'I’ll just stand so tall,'
While violets giggle, 'Let’s bring them all!'
With each little smirk and each playful tease,
The petals persuade with absolute ease!

So if you stroll past this stage of the bloom,
You’ll witness a comedy, dispelling the gloom.
In the garden of laughter, where fun’s on display,
Petals will charm you in their whimsical way!

**The Echoing Fern**

In the shade where ferns do twirl,
A secret dance, a leafy swirl.
They whisper jokes to passing bees,
“Can you handle all this greenery, please?”

The ferns, they chuckle, stretch their fronds,
Cackling at the buttercups' blondes.
With laughter echoing through the woods,
They throw a party, serving good foods.

The owls hoot their own funny tunes,
While squirrels make moves like cartoon loons.
The woodland's rich with glee, oh sweet!
Join the ferns for a leafy treat!

So if you wander past the glen,
Tip your hat to that green crew, then.
For laughter grows beneath the sun,
In the world where ferns have fun!

## Heartbeats of the Harvest

A carrot dreams of being tall,
While potatoes prepare for the fall.
"Look at me!" cries a cheeky pea,
"I'm the best friend for your cup of tea!"

The cabbages gossip over the fence,
"They think we're dull, but we're quite dense!"
Radishes throw a spicy dance,
While tomatoes flaunt in their red pants.

A pumpkin grins, "I'm quite the catch,
At Halloween, they'll put me on a patch!"
As corn kernels pop with pride,
In the harvest, fun will abide!

So let's toast to the fields so bold,
With jokes of harvests yet untold.
The garden's rhythm is hard to resist,
Join the fun, it's hard to miss!

## A Dirge for the Dandelions

Dandelions wail, "Why the frown?
We bloom like gold all over town!"
But in the lawn, the neighbors moan,
"Why can't you stay in your own zone?"

The bees, they buzz, with laughter shared,
"Dandelion, you're not impaired!"
With seeds that float like wishes on air,
Fleeting dreams—we've souls to spare.

Each blow to send a wish out wide,
"Please don't eat me, let me glide!"
Yet here comes a child with a laughter bright,
Who blows the seeds and takes flight!

So here's to blooms that cause a scene,
With tiny wishes in shades of green.
Giggling, dandelions take their call,
In the garden, we embrace them all!

## The Aria of the Arbor

Beneath the trees, where squirrels play,
The branches twist in a grand ballet.
Leaves rustle with secrets they've found,
While nuts drop down with a mighty sound.

The tallest oak, with arms outspread,
Sings tales of glory from years ahead.
"The wind is my friend, come dance along,
Join the forest choir, for we are strong!"

The flowers sway to a funky beat,
With petals twirling, oh so sweet.
"Why you down? Let's paint the ground,
With colors vibrant, life's all around!"

So gather 'round this leafy scene,
Where nature's laughter reigns supreme.
From roots to crowns, we're never alone,
In the aria of trees we've grown!

## The Legend of the Luminous Lily

Once there stood a lily bright,
Her glow could scare away the night.
With petals soft and leaves so green,
She danced like stars, a garden queen.

The bees would buzz, all in a fuss,
For every flower, they'd make a bus.
The lily laughed, with roots so deep,
While nearby hedgehogs softly sleep.

But one fine day, with blooms so bold,
A rabbit claimed her glow as gold.
He wore a crown, so shiny rare,
The lily sighed, 'That's quite a flair!'

Yet soon the moon began to hide,
The rabbit lost his bling with pride.
The lily winked, she knew the score,
While all the critters laughed and swore.

## Whimsy in the Wildflower Wind

In a field where flowers swayed,
A dandelion made a braid.
He twisted stems, with much delight,
His friends all giggled at the sight.

A butterfly joined, dressed up for show,
In polka dots and shades of glow.
Together they pranced, a merry pair,
Twirling blooms through fragrant air.

But then a gust came whirling past,
And sent their fancy plans out fast.
They tumbled down, a floral mess,
While sunflowers watched, with gentle jest.

Yet in the dirt, with all the flurry,
They found new friends, and no more worry.
With every laugh and giggle loud,
In wildflower beds, they felt so proud.

## The Narrative of Nightshade's Glow

Once a nightshade, deep and sly,
Thought she could catch a wandering fly.
With berries bright, she set a trap,
But every insect took a nap.

“Oh my!” she sighed, “How can this be?
I grow in shade, but oh, so free!”
The beetles laughed, her plans unglued,
For all her tricks were just plain shrewd.

A curious frog hopped by one day,
He found her plot quite in dismay.
With big, round eyes, he croaked with cheer,
“Your glowing charms can’t bring them near!”

Nightshade grinned, with a clever wink,
“Maybe it’s time for a new link.”
She baked a treat, and set a feast,
Inviting all, both wild and least.

## A Waltz Among the Wild Ferns

In a shady patch where ferns would twirl,
They danced around, such life they'd swirl.
With spiraled leaves, they formed a line,
And fluffed their fronds like they were fine.

A waltz with wind blew through the trees,
The squirrels joined, as spry as bees.
With acorns tossed to keep the beat,
They turned the forest into a treat.

Then came a snail with quite the shell,
He claimed, "I can dance just as well!"
But when he tried, he slipped and flopped,
The ferns just laughed till daylight stopped.

Yet hearts were light, the fun was grand,
With every twist, they twirled and spanned.
In leafy laughter, friendships grew,
In wild fern waltzes, dreams came true.

## The Rhythm of Roots

In the soil, the roots waltz bright,
Dancing 'neath the moon's soft light.
Wiggling worms join the embrace,
While daisies giggle in their place.

Moles in tuxedos dig with flair,
Singing songs of garden care.
The daisies wear a crown of dew,
And tulips toast the morning brew.

Roses blush at their own jest,
Push up from dirt, they feel so blessed.
The sun, a jokester, throws its rays,
Tickling leaves in a sunny maze.

When the rain drops in a fit,
Rainbows shine and nature's lit.
Even weeds crack a smile or two,
Making mischief just for you.

## Starlit Petals

At night, the flowers start to sway,
In moonlit gowns, they laugh and play.
Petals turn to twinkling stars,
Holding court with little jars.

Ladybugs wear tiny shoes,
Join the dance without a bruise.
While butterflies, those flitting fools,
Try to follow all the rules.

Crickets chirp a wild refrain,
Playing tunes in the weather vein.
Dandelions puff and giggle,
As ants all bust a little wiggle.

And so the garden spins around,
With whispered jokes on fragrant ground.
In this wild fest, all take flight,
Where petals twirl through the night.

## Ode to the Verdant Veil

In the garden, a cloak of green,
Draped over veggies, quite the scene.
Lettuce poses as a model,
While carrots try to hit the throttle.

Spinach flexes its leafy arms,
Claiming strength with silly charms.
Tomatoes blush; they feel so rad,
Though they know they're really bad!

A rabbit hops in to take a peek,
Wearing shades, it looks quite chic.
But with a snap, the cabbage sighs,
As onion's tears begin to rise.

Yet amidst the laughter, roots grow deep,
In this place where secrets keep.
The verdant veil, a joyful sight,
Telling tales in morning light.

## Sonnet of the Seasons

Spring arrives with a sunny grin,
As flowers bloom, the fun begins.
Each petal whispers a silly joke,
While frogs perform on leafy oak.

Summer sizzles with a fruity cheer,
The veggies blush; oh dear, oh dear!
Sunflowers stand like guards at play,
While tomatoes sunbathe every day.

Autumn dances in a sprightly way,
Leaves like confetti start to sway.
Pumpkins giggle with orange glee,
As squirrels plot their winter spree.

Winter's chill brings snowflakes' lace,
And evergreens don a frosty face.
Yet under snow, the laughter stirs,
Nature's jest will soon return.

## The Melody of Mossy Glades

In the glades where mosses play,
Lizards dance without delay.
Fungi wear a silly hat,
While squirrels chat and sit like that.

A worm conducted with great flair,
Sings to flowers, soft and rare.
The sunbeam joins the mossy cheer,
And laughter bubbles everywhere.

Oh, the toadstools giggle bright,
As critters join the wild delight.
In this green and jolly land,
Nature's jesters take a stand.

So come and join this merry crew,
Where everything's a joke that's true.
In the mossy glades of green,
The funniest sights you've ever seen.

## The Symphony of Springs

In springs where water's gurgle grows,
The frogs wear ties as everyone knows.
Crickets play a lively tune,
While flowers clap beneath the moon.

A snail on stage takes a long bow,
While daisies giggle, 'Oh, wee wow!'
The bubbles pop, the ripples dance,
And chubby goldfish join the prance.

Bumblebees are the conductors,
Buzzing loud like playful ruckſters.
With every splash and every leap,
The symphony will make you weep!

So join this lively, silly scene,
Where every drop makes nature keen.
In springs of laughter, none will shy,
With a wink from nature, oh my my!

## The Forest's Folklore

In the forest thick and tall,
Trees tell tales both loud and small.
A wise old owl gives a wink,
'Trust the trees; they can't even drink!'

The rabbits rave with joy so grand,
Singing songs that fill the land.
The bushes blush with berry might,
While shadows giggle in delight.

Deer wear tutus, twirl with grace,
While raccoons boast of treasure space.
This woodland tale is full of fun,
Where mushrooms plot to outdo the sun!

So gather 'round and hear the lore,
Of antics bold forevermore.
In forests deep, with smiles to share,
This quirky life is beyond compare.

## The Ballad of the Basil

In the garden where herbs abound,
Basil's voice is the creamiest sound.
He struts around with leafy flair,
'Smell me now! I'm beyond compare!'

Thyme sings low, with a whispering breeze,
While rosemary blows kisses with ease.
'Why so serious?' basil will shout,
'Let's dance with the garlic and cut out the doubt!'

The chili pepper joins the jig,
As herbs gather round for a big ol' gig.
With every twirl and every spin,
They laugh and play; let the feast begin!

So come and taste this zesty song,
In the garden where we all belong.
With basil leading, bright and spry,
Every meal's a party; oh, my, oh my!

## Whirling Vines

Witty tendrils twist and twirl,
With giggles and a dizzy swirl.
They sneak and sneak, then take a leap,
In the garden, secrets they keep.

A dancing pea, so spry and bright,
Flips through petals, oh what a sight!
A giddy grape with laughter loud,
Makes a toast to every crowd!

## A Lullaby of Lilacs

Oh lilac breeze, with purple cheer,
Whispers sweet secrets in your ear.
Petals sway like giggling sprites,
Under the watch of starry nights.

They hum a tune, soft and light,
Tickling noses, what a delight!
In slumber sweet, come dream and play,
With lilac love to light the way.

## The Epic of Enchanted Evergreens

Tall and proud, the pines stand still,
With stories of mischief, never ill.
They wear their needles like a crown,
Poking clouds while sporting gowns.

A squirrel dressed as a tiny knight,
Defends his acorn day and night.
With laughter shaking every limb,
The trees sway, their joy not dim.

## Swaying in the Summer Breeze

The daisies dance, the sun shines bright,
Tickling grasses in pure delight.
With every gust, a chuckle flows,
As petals partake in breezy shows.

Butterflies burst in colors bold,
Telling tales of spring untold.
With every flap, they spin and twirl,
Creating chaos in a floral whirl.

## Fables in Fragrance

In the garden of giggles, a flower did prance,
With petals so silly, it led a strange dance.
It tickled the bees, made the gardener sneeze,
While daisies rolled laughter, like leaves in the breeze.

A rose tried a joke, but thorns got in the way,
It bloomed with such flair, yet had nothing to say.
The orchids wore hats, quite absurd, it's agreed,
While tulips sipped tea, with extravagant greed.

Down by the pond, a lily sang loud,
Its voice cracked like thunder, it drew quite a crowd.
The frogs popped their eyes, for such a grand show,
While snails made a bet on who'd steal the next glow.

So if you find flowers, all wearing a grin,
Just know that they're laughing at life's little spin.
For in gardens of humor, where colors collide,
The tales weaves on petals; just laugh and abide.

## Gathering Gossamer

In the grove where the fables flutter and fly,
A spider weaved stories that made moths cry.
Each thread spun with glee, each knot tied with care,
A comedic delight, floating light in the air.

The daisies grew dizzy, with laughter so bright,
Swaying to the rhythm of a breezy delight.
While violets whispered their secrets at night,
They shared quite the giggle beneath starlit light.

A butterfly grinned, with a wink and a tease,
It told all the blooms to shimmy and wheeze.
A dance of the petals, a show so divine,
With humor and fragrance, all vines intertwine.

Let nature be merry, let flowers rejoice,
For in playful whispers, the garden finds voice.
Each bloom is a story, each leaf has a score,
In this funny old world, there's always room for more.

## The Twilight Timbers

In the woods where the twilight played hide-and-seek,
Trees wore cheeky grins, as if playing a trick.
The owls danced in circles, with feathers awry,
While fireflies giggled, just buzzing on by.

A squirrel stole acorns, made hats for his friends,
They chuckled and chattered, as laughter transcends.
The pines shared tall tales, of storms they had braved,
All the branches were shaking, the understory waved.

A rabbit wore glasses, quite wise and absurd,
He taught all the critters, with knowledge unheard.
With every small quip, the laughter would grow,
As the twilight timbers put on quite a show.

So wander through shadows, where humor's entwined,
In the heart of the forest, there's joy to be mined.
Every leaf sings a chorus, each trunk holds a jest,
In twilight's embrace, nature's laughter is best.

**The Elysium of Everbloom**

In a realm where the flowers hold court on the hill,
Petunias in gowns danced with unmatched skill.
While violets giggled, they juggled the dew,
And roses played poker, quite mischievous too.

An elderflower whispered a secret to bees,
While sunflowers strutted, as proud as you please.
They shared their own stories of love and of bloom,
In a laughter-filled garden, no trace of gloom.

The fragrances mingled, so sweet and so bright,
As daisies held court in the soft morning light.
With petals like banners, they waved in delight,
Each bloom held a punchline, all ready to bite.

In this joyous haven, let worries take flight,
For every green heart sits within this delight.
In the Elysium of bloom, where laughter will loom,
Remember, dear friend, there's always room for bloom.

## Blooming Ballads

A flower danced with a bee,
Said, "You sting, but you're not mean!"
The tulips giggled in delight,
As roses blushed under the light.

A daffodil wore a sunny hat,
While daisies played the tambourine flat.
Sunflowers spun around in glee,
"Keep buzzing, friend, come dance with me!"

The violets told a pun so clever,
"We bloom in spring—that's now or never!"
With laughter ringing through the field,
Each petal a secret, playfully revealed.

So in this garden, joy abounds,
Where silliness in blossoms resounds.
Among the green, there's always cheer,
In the land where the flowers steer!

## The Language of Leaves

The leaves whispered secrets at dusk,
"Silly breeze, stop making us bust!"
They chattered about the sun's soft glow,
And how it made their colors show.

A leaf turned red, it felt so grand,
"I'm a maple, King of the Land!"
Yet a little olive waved with pride,
"Don't leaf me out, just let it slide!"

The whispering leaves, a drama they spun,
About rival branches, who's number one.
They giggled and gossiped in the light,
As the stars came to witness their slight.

So next time you wander in the wood,
Listen closely; you'll find it's good.
Nature has stories that weave and twine,
In every leaf, a tale to shine!

## Garden's Gentle Echo

In the garden, whispers roam,
A snail declared, "I’ll find my home!"
The daisies chuckled as they grew,
“Oh, hurry up, we’re laughing at you!”

A worm lost his way in the mud,
"I think I’ll ask that flower for a bud!"
While crickets played a lively tune,
With petals twirling like a festive balloon.

The herbs held a party, fresh and spry,
Cilantro yelled, "Let’s give it a try!"
As basil waltzed with parsley near,
The garden erupted in joyful cheer!

So if you’re feeling low today,
Just stroll through flora, hear them play.
Their giggles echo in sunshine bright,
A garden’s laughter, pure delight!

## Lament of the Lush

Oh, the grass sang songs of the past,
"So much rain, we grew up fast!"
The ferns sighed, longing for sun,
"Too much shade, this isn't fun!"

A cactus queried, "What's your plight?"
"I need space, but you're too tight!"
The lilies groaned from muddy ground,
"Give us chance, let joy abound!"

A charming pot stood all alone,
"My flowers bloom, but I'm on loan!"
The vines teased, "You'll never be free,
For tenants tight with joy's decree!"

Though they lament, it's all in jest,
For in this lush, they find their nest.
With banter light and passions flush,
They bloom together, bold and lush!

## Rhythms of Rebirth

Seeds pop up in a fray,
Dancing in the light of day.
Plants in costumes, all a-show,
Whispering secrets to the snow.

Frogs in flip-flops leap around,
While daisies join them—what a sound!
The sun winks at the merry trees,
As they sway and shake in the breeze.

Breezy blooms hum a tune,
Singing softly to the moon.
Buds burst forth with giggles loud,
As pollen draws a playful crowd.

Nature's prance, a jester's call,
With rascally leaves that rise and fall.
Join the fun, don't just sit!
In this garden, life's a wit!

## A Ballad for the Briar

Oh, briar rose, so thorny and wild,
Clumsy bees make the bees smile.
You hug the fence with prickly grace,
In your briar patch, what a place!

The vagrants seek to dance with you,
But get stuck in what you do.
You laugh and bloom, a secret glow,
As the clumsy folks come and go.

Upon a daring dare, you tease,
With petals open to the breeze.
While hapless souls, in laughter bound,
Roll away from where they're found.

So here's to you, dear briar friend,
Your playful thorns we don't expend.
For every laugh, a flower bright,
In your thorny sphere, pure delight!

## The Cadence of the Corm

Dancing corms with roots so stout,
Wiggle wiggle, without doubt.
Beneath the soil, they gather cheer,
Cracking jokes only they can hear.

Silly sprouts stretch high for fun,
And twirl ‘round just like the sun.
The corms conspire with stealthy sneer,
As neighbors wonder what they hear.

Oh, cheerful bulbs, such mischief-makers,
Chasing down the garden's shakers.
In this patch, no frown should stay,
The corms ensure it’s a zany day.

As roots entwine in jolly jest,
Let plants unite for this great quest.
In jokes and blooms, they find their form,
Spreading laughter like a warm storm!

## An Elegy for Endangered Flora

From petals lost to time's cruel hand,
Migrates the tale of a flower band.
With melancholy, they wish to play,
Yet vanished blooms have gone away.

“We were here once!” they long to yell,
In every breeze, they weave their spell.
Yet humans trample, growling loud,
Forgetting joys in a bustling crowd.

The orchids hid, a sneaky game,
While ferns, though shy, feel the same.
Yet in a garden, there lies a chance,
To share their tale, to laugh, to dance.

So let’s revive the flora fair,
In silly songs, let’s take great care.
For laughter blooms ‘neath every sun,
Together we can all be one!

## Ballad of the Blossoms

In a garden where daisies dance,
Bumblebees wear a polka dot pants.
Roses giggle in shades of pink,
While sunflowers (oh!) can hardly think.

Daffodils hum a jolly tune,
As violets whisper to the moon.
Tulips teasing with color bright,
Claim that bees are a silly sight.

In this wacky floral parade,
Every stem has a joke made.
Laughter blooms from roots below,
As petals flutter to and fro.

So come, join this leafy spree,
Where every flower's wild and free!
With nature's laugh, it's hard to frown,
In this garden of the gown and crown.

## Verses Beneath the Vines

Underneath the tangled green,
A sly snake thought he was unseen.
But grapes giggled, oh what a view,
As he slithered past in his shoe.

The ivy laughed, making it clear,
That being sneaky is quite a fear.
Chickadees chirp with a cheeky fight,
While frogs leap in the soft moonlight.

With every twist of mingled roots,
The vines play games in leafy suits.
A dapper snail with a hat so fine,
Tries to dance, but can’t quite align.

In this viney realm of good cheer,
Laughter echoes, loud and clear.
So grab a drink from a bushy vine,
And join the fun—ain't life divine?

## The Tapestry of Tulips

Tulips in a dazzling array,
Wink at each other throughout the day.
In shades so wild, they strut and sway,
Making fun of the bees' ballet.

One sprightly bloom in a tutu bright,
Challenges a daisy for a dance tonight.
While lilly pads float down a stream,
Frogs croak: “Life’s a beautiful dream!”

Petals play hide and seek in the sun,
With laughter as they twirl and run.
They tell jokes to the butterflies,
As colors mingle beneath blue skies.

Tightly knit in a flowery plot,
These tulips know laughter matters a lot.
So sway along in the garden's gleam,
Where petals burst forth with a hearty scream!

## Melodies of the Moss

Beneath the trees where mosses cling,
Frogs hold concerts, they love to sing.
With nature's rhythm and a croaky croon,
They jam all week, by the light of the moon.

The moss waltzes on the dampened ground,
While squirrels join in with a funny sound.
An old snail plays with a funky beat,
As fireflies dance by the mossy seat.

Every patch tells secrets of old,
As lichen laughs, daring and bold.
With a splash, the raindrops add to the cheer,
While mushrooms chuckle, spreading good fear!

In the realm where green things play,
Each note of laughter makes the day.
So join the chorus, just don't get lost,
In the magic where fun is the cost.

## Rhymes of Regrowth

When plants do dance in the springtime light,
They sway and twirl, it’s quite a sight!
The daisies giggle, the ferns take flight,
In the greenest garden, all feels right.

A cactus winks with spikes so bold,
Telling tales, or so I’m told.
A rose rolls its eyes, as stories unfold,
While sunflowers gossip in the sun’s warm gold.

The weeds play tricks, it's all a game,
While laughing leaves call each other names.
In this playful world, nothing’s the same,
Botanical fun, with joy we proclaim!

So raise your spade and whisper a cheer,
For those silly plants that thrive without fear.
Let’s celebrate nature with laughter near,
In the dance of the garden, the fun is clear!

## The Serenade of the Saplings

Oh little saplings, standing so spry,
You wiggle your leaves as the clouds pass by.
You twirl in the breeze, oh my, oh my!
In this leafy concert, spirits fly high.

With playful roots, they tug and tease,
Beneath the soil, they'll tickle with ease.
While ants march by, busy as bees,
The saplings giggle beneath the trees.

They flirt with the bees in a sweet ballet,
While the dandelions dream and sway.
A chorus of nature singing away,
In the charming woods, we love to play.

So let's join the dance of the saplings small,
With each little leaf, we're having a ball.
In their verdant world, we're having a ball,
Together we'll laugh as the wildflowers call!

## The Poetry of Pollen

Pollen floats like a feather in air,
Drifting along without a care.
It flirts with the flowers, oh so rare,
Whispering secrets, a love affair.

The bees start to buzz, they join the fun,
Collecting the goodies, oh what a run!
While sneezers nearby say, "No more sun!"
Allergies abound, under skies so fun.

Dandelions grin, they're the jokers of grass,
Puffing their seeds like a top-notch class.
While the flowers laugh, as the seasons pass,
In this pollen party, they're first in the mass.

So if you feel sneezy, just take a seat,
And enjoy the show, it's quite a treat!
For pollen's a poet, in summer's heat,
Creating a tale, and life is sweet!

## Ballad of the Bluebells

Bluebells chime with a tinkling sound,
Dancing in meadows, where joy is found.
They wiggle their stems, twirling all around,
In a floral festival, let's gather 'round.

With shades of azure, they paint the ground,
While bees' busy buzzing is quite renowned.
A patch of blue laughter that knows no bound,
In a garden of giggles, enchantment is crowned.

Frogs serenade with a ribbiting song,
As the bluebells sway, wild and strong.
Even the butterflies can't go wrong,
In this whimsical world where we all belong.

So here's to the bluebells, raising a cheer,
For their funny performances, a delight to appear.
In nature's own symphony, we hold dear,
Join the ballad of blooms, let's spread the cheer!

## The Songbird's Soprano in Saplings

In a tiny tree, a bird sings loud,
With a voice that troubles every proud crowd.
The saplings sway, they giggle and sway,
While the songbird thinks it's Broadway today.

The squirrels all dance, they throw a big show,
While the branches shake, and the leaves start to glow.
Each high note adds to their raucous delight,
As sunbeams twinkle, oh what a sight!

Raccoons clap paws, they join the big fun,
Under the moon where antics are spun.
But one wrong move, and it's chaos in flight,
That dapper little bird took off in full fright!

So here in this grove, laughter's the rule,
Where saplings provide a natural school.
For every tree knows, with foliage keen,
That nature's good humor is often unseen.

## The Harmonies of Hemlock and Heather

In the forest of whispers, hemlock stands tall,
While heather just giggles, not caring at all.
They have debates, about the best shade,
But humor's their bond, in the sun they've laid.

The hemlock says, "I'm the coolest around!"
The heather rolls her eyes, sits firmly on ground.
"You may shade the deer, but I'm radiant bloom,"
With petals so vibrant, dispelling the gloom.

A squirrel pops in, saying, "What's all this fuss?"
"You both shine your way, but don't cause a fuss!"
Together they chuckle, it's a raucous retreat,
While birds make the music, a symphonic feat.

With laughter like sunlight that dances on leaves,
Together their joy is what nature weaves.
In harmony's roots, they linger just right,
Making melodies twinkle through day into night.

## Whispers of the Wildflowers

In the meadow where flowers prattle and tease,
Each bloom has its tale, shared on a breeze.
The daisies shout, "Look, we’re the stars!"
While violets snicker, aiming for Mars!

A dandelion giggles, "I’m fluff, I’m supreme!"
While tulips roll their petals, live out a dream.
They gossip and jest, with sunshine as cheer,
Each petal a laugh, every stem draws near.

The bees join the chat, buzzing in rhyme,
While ants march along, keeping perfect time.
In this patch of color, joy fills the air,
Where laughter's the secret, igniting a flare.

So here in this haven, where wildflowers play,
Each moment's a treasure, in their own funny way.
Nature’s comic act, with a flourish so bright,
As petals unfurl beneath soft moonlight.

## Serenade of the Saplings

Three little saplings in a band so tight,
Swaying and dancing through the moonlit night.
Each rustle a tune, as they play and sway,
Beneath the stars, it's a leafy café.

"I'm the tallest!" barks one, with leaves all aglow,
"But I'm the smartest!" the smallest does crow.
With banter so quick, and laughter so wide,
They twirl in a circle, full of leafy pride.

The branches start tickling, a curious game,
While critters all gather, so none feel the same.
Frogs croak a beat, while crickets compose,
The saplings all smile as the laughter flows.

In the grove of whispers, the night becomes bright,
As saplings make music in playful delight.
And with every chuckle, the world feels so grand,
For in nature's embrace, laughter walks hand in hand.

## The Rhapsody of Rainfall on Roses

The raindrops dance on petals bright,
Each one a little dot of light.
Roses giggle, swaying with cheer,
"Come on, let’s have a splashy beer!"

They twirl and sway, a rosy ballet,
As clouds play music, come out and stay.
The thorns are the bouncers, standing so tall,
"No sorrow here! Just laughter for all!"

A butterfly flutters, wearing a grin,
Sipping on nectar, then spinnin’ like a pin.
It’s a party of petals under the sky,
Where roses rave and the spirits fly!

So grab your galoshes, dance in the rain,
Join the floral fest, shake off the mundane!
In the garden of giggles, life’s such a thrill,
With laughter in roses, it’s always a 'will!'

## A Tale Told by Tulips

Oh tulips bright, with colors galore,
They gossip and chat, oh what a rapport!
"Did you see Sophie? She got a new hat!"
"She looks quite snazzy, just like a sprat!"

Springtime mischief, a sight to behold,
Tulips get tipsy when sunlight unfolds.
Swinging their heads, they wiggle and weave,
"Let's throw a dance party! Who needs to grieve?"

One tulip declared, "I'll wear a bow tie!"
"Not too shabby! Just let out a sigh!"
Through petals and petals, their laughter balloons,
In fields of delight, they sing silly tunes.

So grab that bouquet, come join the fun,
In the tulip's tale, there's room for everyone!
With petals as banners, they march in a line,
In this jolly garden, all spirits align!

## The Epiphany of Edible Weeds

Wandering weeds, once thought to be pests,
Decided to show they can be the best.
"We're more than a nuisance! We're tasty indeed!"
"Have a bite of this, just follow our lead!"

Dandelions chuckle, all yellow and bright,
"In salads or tea, we're such a delight!"
Clover chimes in, with a wink and a grin,
"Just try us in stews, let the fun begin!"

So farmer and chef, they gathered in awe,
Forgotten are weeds, now adored like a law.
Each leaf a treasure, each stem a delight,
Making munchies fun, oh what a sight!

Eating the weeds, what a crafty affair,
They giggle and munch without any care.
So here's to the greens, with humor they splurge,
In salad or soup, they joyfully emerge!

## The Saga of the Saffron Sky

Oh, the sun sets low, casting gold in the air,
Crocuses peek out, without a single care.
"Life's a grand canvas, let’s splash it with cheer!"
"Saffron skies call, let’s paint it here, dear!"

The daisies nod, in their white and their gold,
"Artistry blooms, let the magic unfold!"
While sunflowers stretch, standing proud and tall,
"Let’s twirl with the sunset, a festival ball!"

There’s laughter and whimsy, a pastel display,
The flowers compete, for the brightest bouquet.
With petals like confetti, the sky shows off flair,
A saffron delight, floating free in the air!

So dance in the dusk, as the colors collide,
Join the floral fandango, with blooms as your guide!
In this saga of sunsets, all flowers unite,
Under saffron horizons, everything’s right!

## The Chime of Cherry Blossoms

Cherry trees in bloom so bright,
Dance all day, a funny sight.
Bees buzzing loud, a merry crew,
Sipping nectar, what a view!

Petals fall like pink confetti,
While squirrels scamper, oh so petty.
They plot their heists with crafty flair,
In search of snacks, they're quite the pair!

Lovers stroll with smiles so wide,
Tripping over roots, they glide.
The trees just giggle, swaying free,
Nature's jesters, can't you see?

A springtime cheer, let's raise a toast,
To cherry blooms we love the most!
With laughter ringing in the air,
Let's dance beneath, without a care!

## The Dialogue of Dappled Light

Sunbeams play on leaves so bright,
Whispering secrets, oh what a sight!
Frogs croak jokes from the pond's green throne,
While butterflies chuckle, never alone.

A rabbit hops with comedic flair,
Telling tales, but who would care?
The flowers giggle, swaying by,
'Oh, look at that, he thinks he's spry!'

Mossy giants grumble in shade,
'Young ones these days are so poorly made!'
Yet every quip, a leafy jest,
Nature's humor is simply the best.

As shadows dance in the dappled light,
The forest hosts a joyful night.
Come join the laughter, feel the rhyme,
In this quirky world, we pass the time!

## A Soprano of Sprouts

Tiny sprouts with voices bright,
Sing in harmony, pure delight.
With glee, they poke through earthy beds,
Chorusing songs, ‘We’re sprouting heads!’

Carrots hum, while radishes sway,
Lettuce leads the merry ballet.
They twirl and dip, oh what a scene,
Veggie cavaliers, all dressed in green!

Tomatoes blush, feeling quite grand,
While beans tango, hand in hand.
The whole garden chuckles, full of cheer,
As nature's choir draws you near.

And when the sun bids day goodbye,
The sprouts all yawn with a sleepy sigh.
But tomorrow they'll wake with songs so sweet,
In their lively world, no chance of defeat!

## Shadows Under the Magnolia

Under magnolia, shadows play,
Frogs debate who'll hop today.
In hushed tones they share their dreams,
While a wise snail plots, or so it seems.

Petals drift like whispered tales,
As bees weave songs, where laughter prevails.
A sit-and-stare contest ensues,
With a grumpy pup, who just can't snooze.

The breeze is cheeky, tickling leaves,
While a lazy worm spins yarns, it weaves.
All join in, under the bloom,
Creating giggles, dispelling gloom.

When twilight falls, they gather 'round,
Sharing each laugh, joyous sounds.
For in this place, of light and shade,
Friendship flourishes, never to fade!

## The Overture of Orchids

In a garden not far, where the orchids bloom,
They shimmy and sway, clearing all the gloom.
With petals like skirts, they twirl with delight,
In the sun's warm embrace, they dance day and night.

A bee joins the fun with a buzz and a spin,
He dives for the nectar, a sweet life to win.
The orchids just chuckle, in colors so bright,
While hummingbirds hover, a charming sight!

They throw a grand party, all flowers invited,
Daisies and daisies, all wildly excited.
The joke's on the weeds, they're stuck in the mud,
While orchids sip dew from their porcelain bud.

With laughter and cheer, they serenade bees,
Their notes like a fragrance that dances on breeze.
The world might just frown, and its troubles endure,
But orchids will giggle, and that's for sure!

## Whistling Weeds

In the backyard where grass grows incredibly wild,
The weeds start a chorus like a mischievous child.
They whistled at daisies, who gasped in surprise,
Saying, "Join our parade, forget your prim ties!"

With roots as their trumpets and leaves growing long,
They danced through the garden, creating a song.
A dandelion's fluff flew, tickling the air,
As the weeds laughed out loud without a single care.

They fashioned a band with a thistle for beat,
A clover on drums, oh what a treat!
But the lawnmower crept in with a dreadful intention,
And the weeds broke the jam, jumping in apprehension.

But as blades of green fell, they snickered and cheered,
"We may be short-lived, but we've not disappeared!
In every crack, and every little crevice,
We'll rise up again, and oh how we'll relish!

## The Cadence of Cacti

In a desert so dry, where the cacti stand tall,
They sway to the rhythm, not afraid at all.
Their prickly personas are always a jest,
In the land of confusion, they're clearly the best.

With arms raised up high, they reach for the sun,
"Catch us if you can!" they say, having fun.
The lizards roll by, with a grin and a wink,
Joining the dance, they'll cause quite a stink!

A saguaro said, "Hey, I'll tell you a tale,
Of a tortoise who tried to steal cactus ale!"
Laughter erupted, oh, what a delight,
As they swayed and whispered all through the night.

In the moonlit glow, all the shadows did prance,
As the cacti hummed softly, inviting a chance.
To be spiky and funny, oh such a delight,
They held a grand fiesta under stars shining bright!

## The Verse of Violets

In a patch of pure purple, the violets sing,
With giggles and chuckles, oh, such a sweet thing!
They sway to a tune that the bumblebees hum,
And share all their secrets on how to have fun.

A violet named Vera said, “What’s in a name?”
When everything’s blooming, it’s all just a game!
With petals like velvet and fragrance galore,
They float on the breeze, always wanting more.

They tangle with daisies, they poke and they prod,
Injuring no one, just giving a nod.
“Why grow up to worry, when you can stay small?
We’ll spin and we’ll giggle, for life’s just a ball!”

And when the sun sets, casting gold on their scene,
The violets are dreaming of next spring's green.
With laughter and joy, they bloom and confuse,
For violets love to play hide and seek too!

## Chorus of the Canopy

In the treetops, branches sway,
Squirrels dance and laugh all day,
Leaves are clapping in a cheer,
While birds crack jokes that all can hear.

The sun peeks down with a bright grin,
Saying, "Hey, where do I begin?"
The flowers giggle, "Right on cue!"
Breeze joins in with a lovely woo!

Little bugs form a marching band,
Playing tunes throughout the land,
While ants perform a comedy,
In a tiny, wild cacophony!

As night falls, the stars take bets,
On who will win the garden sets,
With humor blooming everywhere,
The forest stage is filled with flair!

## The Flower's Fable

Once a rose, in shades of red,
Dreamed of a crown upon its head,
But bees just buzzed and tossed their tunes,
"You're better off with your perfume!"

A daisy piped in with a giggle,
"Life's too short for any wiggle!"
The tulip teased with a playful sway,
"Let's dance and play the day away!"

Then came a pouty little sprout,
"I wish I had a fun way out!"
But petals cheered with laughter bright,
"Just bloom where planted, that's your light!"

And thus, a fable starts to bloom,
Where joy and color chase the gloom,
For in the garden's funny tale,
Every flower has a chance to sail!

## Rooted Reverie

In the soil, roots tell a joke,
"We're grounded, but never broke!"
Worms are laughing underground,
As whispers of humor abound.

A fern chimed in with a wise quip,
"Life's a vine, take every trip!"
While daisies rolled, with glee they said,
"Let's have a party, who's up for bread?"

The cacti spiked with witty jests,
"Stay hydrated, avoid the pests!"
A silly gourd claimed it was grand,
"To grow a belly from all this sand!"

In the roots, the laughter swirls,
With every sprout, a tale unfurls,
For every laugh beneath the ground,
Is where true joy is always found!

## The Song of the Sunlit Stems

Oh, the stems sway to and fro,
In sunlight's glow, they steal the show,
Each one hums a tune so bright,
Under the watchful eye of light.

"Hello, flower! What’s the deal?"
"Just soaking rays, it's quite the meal!"
Sunflowers turn their heads around,
Chasing smiles without a sound.

Petunias giggle, swaying near,
“Let’s throw a picnic, gather here!”
With lemonade made from morning dew,
And snacks supplied by the busy crew!

So let the garden laugh and play,
With sunlit stems paving the way,
For in this lively, vibrant stream,
Each little plant fulfills a dream!

## The Dance of Dandelion Dreams

In the breeze, they sway with cheer,
Little yellow suns appear.
They twirl and spin in wild delight,
Dancing with all their might.

A gust of wind, and off they fly,
Seeds like tiny kites in the sky.
Chasing clouds and racing birds,
Singing sweet and silly words.

With every puff, they laugh and shout,
Watch me scatter, there's no doubt!
To lands unknown, their laughter spreads,
Oh, the joy that dandelion threads!

But here comes the mower, oh dear me!
It’s a dance of haste, not jubilee.
Sliced and diced, their day is done,
Yet still, they smile, “That was fun!”

## A Chorus of Blossoms

Petals pink and petals white,
Gather round in morning light.
Singing loud of springtime's glee,
"Who has the best perfume?" says she.

"Roses, please!" a daisy cried,
"Nature's royalty, we can't hide!"
Sunshine giggled with a ray,
"Flowers, bloom and steal the day!"

Lilies chimed, "Don't be so vain,
Anything in purple reigns!"
A bumblebee buzzed in to say,
"Stop the chatter, it's time to play!"

With a buzz and bloom, what a show,
Around the garden, laughter flows.
Each petal whispers, full of pride,
A little rhyme cannot subside!

## Serenade of the Silent Sprout

In the corner, green and shy,
A sprout peeks up to say hi.
“I may be small, but I've got flair,
Watch me dance without a care!”

Roots are jiving, leaves make a scene,
Photosynthesis? It's a machine!
Twisting, turning, in pure delight,
They laugh at shadows creeping at night.

“Oh look, a worm!” the sprout exclaims,
“Come join my wiggly, earthy games!”
A party starts beneath the ground,
With soil confetti all around!

Though the world above seems quite so grand,
This little sprout has a fun-filled plan.
With every inch, it’s sure to shout,
Who needs fame? I’m all about clout!

## Verses of the Verdant Veil

In the garden, green and bright,
Leaves are whispering, what a sight!
"Did you hear the gossip today?"
"All the old herbs are in dismay!"

Thyme declared, with sass and flair,
"Without me, dinner's a total scare!"
Rosemary chuckled, "Oh don't you fret,
My perfume's the best, I'll bet!"

They traded jokes as sunlight poured,
While flowers waltzed, slightly bored.
"Can you get a salad going?"
"Silly greens, they're the ones knowing!"

As evening falls, they laugh still more,
With breezy tunes and a garden score.
Together they hum, a leafy song,
In this verdant world, they all belong!

www.ingramcontent.com/pod-product-compliance
Lightning Source LLC
Chambersburg PA
CBHW071854160426
43209CB00003B/558
* 9 7 8 1 8 0 5 6 7 0 3 5 3 *